Dyslexia:
The creative genius

Diversity does not mean inferiority.
Comprehensive guide to discovering the
strengths of dyslexic children

Helen Parent

0 1 0
1 1 1
1 0 0
0 0 1
        0
0 1 1
  1 0
0
1 0 0
    1
1 0
    0
        1
1   1

1   0
    0   1
  1 0
0 0 1
    1
0 1
        0
0   1
    1
    0
1
0
1

"Everyone is a genius. But if you judge a fish by its ability to climb a tree, it will live its whole life believing that it is stupid."

Albert Einstein

| Gustave FLAUBERT | HANS CHRISTIAN ANDERSEN | Agatha CHRISTIE | Edgar Allan POE | Ernest HEMINGWAY | Victor HUGO |

| Michelangelo | Vincent VAN GOGH | Ludwig van BEETHOVEN | Léonard de VINCI | MOZART | Pablo Ruiz PICASSO |

| _Louis PASTEUR | Albert EINSTEIN | Benjamin FRANKLIN | Alexandre GRAHAM BELL | Thomas EDISON | GALILEE |

| John F. KENNEDY | Winston CHURCHILL | Bill GATES | William R. HEWLETT | Ted TURNER | Richard BRANSON |

| Steven SPIELBERG | Jack NICHOLSON | Robin WILLIAMS | Tom CRUISE | Hugues AUFRAY | WALT DISNEY |

| Jacky STEWART | Auguste RODIN | Nathalie Baye | Mika | Orlando BLOOM | Keira KNIGHTLEY | Patrick Dempsey |

TABLE OF CONTENTS

110 1 1001110011 11110011 0
001
100
0 0
110
1 0
1
1 1
011
0
101
000
111
10
11
01
1

dysfunction *noun* ...
tioning. ■ **dysfuncti**...
dyslexia *noun, psych*...
difficulty in readin...
■ **dyslexic** *adj, noun*...
...menorrhoea

INTRODUCTION

Through this book, I would like you to rediscover what is most beautiful behind a dyslexic subject. Specifically: do you know what Leonardo da Vinci and Walt Disney had in common? They were dyslexic and had the gift of creativity and imagination. Yet we seem to forget this or perhaps even don't know it. Yet movies like 'Stars on Earth' should remind us that all it takes is just a little extra attention, and a little love and that is how what we think of as a 'problem,' will become a magnificent discovery.

Through the various chapters, I will address the salient features of Dyslexia.

In Chapter One I will discuss what we mean when we talk about Dyslexia, what definitions over time have been given, and the link to specific learning disorders (SAD).

In Chapter Two, on the other hand, I will go on to

examine the personality of the dyslexic individual, thus his or her creative potential, also referring to the great dyslexics of the past and present, such as Napoleon Bonaparte, Emile Zola, Steven Spielberg, Isaac Newton, and many others.

Finally, in Chapter 4, I will discuss one dyslexic, in particular, Ronald Davis, who after a childhood marked by learning difficulties, thanks to his 'gift' realized, only at the age of thirty-eight, that he had the ability to read at an absolutely astonishing speed. This led him to develop a revolutionary new method for correcting dyslexia and learning disorders in general. All encapsulated in his volume 'The Gift of Dyslexia.

Teachers, in order to accept a child with reading difficulties as dyslexic, ask him to be a little Einstein, forgetting that even Einstein's teachers did not realize they were dealing with a genius.

4

CHAPTER 1

DYSLEXIA AND SPECIFIC LEARNING DISORDERS.

1.1 Definitions of Dyslexia

S OS Dyslexia' is the call for help launched by contemporary society, where the written language is the opening key to global communication.

Everyone now talks about Dyslexia, some with the expression 'Are you dyslexic?, they indicate in a derogatory and incorrect sense, those who cannot express themselves correctly or stumble over words, and well few know how to give a definition.

To talk about Dyslexia is to talk about reading and writing, processes that become automatic after the first stage of learning. Most children learn to write on their own; in any case, 90 percent of 1st graders learn the alphabetic code in two months, regardless of the teaching method they are exposed to.

However, a small but substantial part of the child population has significant difficulties in learning to read. The beginning of their failure to acquire this skill is marked by early institutions on reading. Not only that.

There are children who also present significant difficulties in spelling, calculations, or everyday actions, simple for us, such as tying their shoes, or shirts. Theirs is a constant war.

This is why they are labeled as listless, lazy, or unintelligent. Instead, they are simply dyslexic.

Few know how to give an adequate definition of what Dyslexia really is. The etiology of the term comes from the Greek *Dys* (difficulty) plus *lexis* (reading). In general, when we refer to the word Dyslexia we indicate difficulty in reading correctly and fluently. In particular, we recognize two types of dyslexia:

❖ Developmental dyslexia: occurs during school age, particularly in the early years when school learning begins; the characteristics of dyslexia may vary in relation to changes related to the child's growth; congenital form affecting children.

❖ Acquired dyslexia: mainly occurs in adults or as a result of injuries that cause difficulty in normal reading ability or related aspects.

Other definitions can be found in the Orton Dyslexia Society (1997) which states that developmental dyslexia is a specific disorder on a linguistic basis, of constitutional origin, characterized by difficulties in decoding single words, often unexpected in relation to age, cognitive and scholastic abilities, not attributable to a generalized developmental disorder or sensory impairment; it manifests itself with large variables of difficulty in different forms of language ability. Not to be forgotten is the one issued by the International Dyslexia Association, which made its contribution by defining developmental dyslexia as a specific learning disability of neurobiological origin: it is characterized by difficulty in performing accurate and/or fluent reading and by poor writing and decoding skills. These difficulties typically result from a deficit in the phonological component of language, often unexpected in relation to other cognitive abilities and the assurance of adequate schooling. Secondary consequences may include reading comprehension problems and reduced reading practice, which may impede vocabulary and general knowledge growth.

Worthy of a separate mention is the research of noted cognitivist neuroscientist Maryanne Wolf, among the most prominent 'brain reading' researchers and a scholar of learning and language disorders such as dyslexia.

Through her studies, she has shown that reading is not a <<natural>> process, which does not rely directly on a genetic program transmitted from one generation to the next.

"Reading can only be learned because of the innate plasticity of our brains, but as soon as a person learns to read, his or her brain changes forever, both physiologically and intellectually." (Maryanna Wolf, We are not born to read)

Wolf asserts that reading is not a natural human aptitude but an invention of man, perhaps the most ingenious of all, dating back 6,000 years to Mesopotamia, with the cuneiform writing of the Sumerians. The development of reading in any kind of written language, involves a readjustment of preexisting structures, the ability to specialize by the neuronal groups in these structures, and the ability, by all these groups and circuits, to retrieve and connect information quickly, thus, automatically.

Therefore, it must be kept in mind that Dyslexia has complex implications:

1. Reading is an extraordinary feat that can be compromised by several obstacles: if a child cannot read fluently enough after the first three months of school and in the absence of vision or hearing problems, he or she should receive an initial evaluation by learning specialists.

2. There is no single form of dyslexia: the difficulties a child may experience are multiple and can affect not only reading but also writing and calculation.

3. The best known difficulties are those involving phonology and reading fluency: therefore, the best predictors of a child's future struggles to learn to read involve phonological awareness and naming speed.

4. One should always assess the child's language: because often, a language disorder is also hidden behind a learning problem.

5. Dyslexia interventions: should aim at the development of each of the components that contribute to reading, from language to spelling.

It would be inappropriate if, however, I stuck to

talking only about Dyslexia, as this belongs to the heterogeneous group of disorders that manifest themselves only in the acquisition of school skills such as reading, writing, and computation, referred to with Specific Learning Disorders, i.e., SAD.

1.2 The correlation between DSA and Dyslexia.

For correct definition of DSA is Specific Learning Disorders and they indicate those neurodevelopmental disorders that affect one of the areas that underlie learning.

For the purposes of the law, the disorders are understood as follows:

❖ Dyslexia: a specific disorder manifested by difficulty in learning to read, particularly in deciphering linguistic signs, that is, in the correctness and speed of reading.

❖ Dysgraphia: a specific writing disorder that manifests itself in difficulty in graphic achievement.

❖ Dysorthography: a specific writing disorder that manifests itself in difficulties in transcoding language processes.

❖ Dyscalculia: a specific disorder that manifests itself in difficulty in the automatisms of calculation and number processing.

These disorders can exist together or separately.

Emphasis must be placed on the importance and necessity of distinguishing between pupils' academic difficulties and learning disorders. While it is very likely that a child with a learning disorder also has school difficulties, the reverse is not necessarily true.

For the classification of ASD, we refer to the major international diagnostic manuals that are used by clinicians, such as the DSM-IV-TR (Diagnostic and Statistical Manual of Mental Disorder) and ICD-10 (the tenth version of the International Classification of Disorders) below with their definitions.

In the DSM-IV-TR, edited by the American Psychiatric Association, ASD fall under the section of Disorders usually first diagnosed in childhood, childhood, or adolescence and specifically under Axis I. Specifically, they are defined as Learning Disorders: "Characterized by school functioning that is substantially lower than would be expected given chronological age, psychometric assessment of intelligence, and age-appropriate education of the subject."

The specific disorders, identified in this section, are:

- ❖ Reading Disorder,
- ❖ Calculation Disorder,

- ❖ Writing Expression Disorder,

- ❖ Learning Disorder Not Otherwise Specified.

According to DSM-IV-TR sixty to eighty percent of people diagnosed with Reading Disorders are male, this is because schools report to services mainly males who in the classroom, unlike females, in association with Learning Disorders, prove to be more restless and problematic in behavior. In fact, this finding balances out when rigorous and scientifically validated diagnostic assessment is used (e.g., screening procedures in elementary school). Regarding association, among these disorders in the manual, it is stated that reading, written expression, and computation disorders are commonly associated and it is rare for any of these to be present without the reading disorder. With respect to the diagnosis of ASD the manual states:

Learning disorders are diagnosed when a child's performance on standardized, individually administered tests on reading, computation, or written expression is significantly below what is expected based on age, education, and intelligence level. They significantly interfere with academic achievement or activities of daily living that require reading, calculation, or writing skills.

In DSM- IV we can find some of the disorders that are associated with ASD, such as a low level of self-esteem and difficulty in relating to others. The manual goes into great detail about the criteria to be used for a differential diagnosis; in fact, children may write poorly, but not always because of a learning disorder.

A subject's poor performance could depend on school difficulties related to a lack of opportunities, poor teaching, or cultural factors, and for this, it is necessary to be sure to rule out its occurrence.

In the International Classification of Syndromes and Behavioral Disorders (ICD- 10), compiled by the WHO, ASD fall under the heading of developmental and specific school skill disorders and is defined as follows:

'Developmental specific school skill disorders include groups of morbid conditions that manifest with specific and relevant learning impairments in school skills. These learning impairments are not the direct result of other disorders, although they may occur simultaneously with the latter conditions. Frequently, these disorders occur together with other kinetic syndromes or with other developmental disorders. The etiology of developmental disorders specific to school skills is not known, but it is assumed that there is the significant intervention of biological factors, which interact with nonbiological factors producing the manifestations'.

Regarding the characteristics of ASD, ICD-10 states that:

'They are disorders in which the normal modes of acquisition of the skills in question are altered early in development. They are not simply a consequence of a lack of opportunity to learn and are not due to an acquired brain disease. Rather, the disorders are believed to result from abnormalities in cognitive processing related largely to some kind of biological dysfunction. As with most other developmental disorders, these conditions are markedly more frequent in males'.

DYSLEXIA

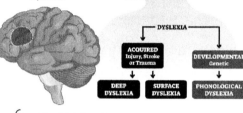

Typical	Dyslexic

Typical {
Broca's Area, Inferior Frontal Gyrus
Articulation - Word Analysis

Parieto-temporal
Word Analysis

Occipito-temporal
Word Form

Dyslexic {
Broca's Area, Inferior Frontal Gyrus
Articulation - Word Analysis

Parieto-temporal
Word Analysis

Occipito-temporal
Word Form

VISION
- Sees text as moving or blurry
- Reverse letters
- Skip words or lines
- Loses place

READING
- Finds reading hard
- Misreads words
- Not fluent
- Doesn't always understand what was read

WRITING
- Poor spelling
- Poor punctuation and grammar
- Difficulty structuring text

MEMORY
- Difficulties with remembering sequences
- Poor working memory

AUDITORY
- Hearing can be distorted
- Difficulty breaking words into sounds

NEURO
- Slow processing speed
- Word finding problems
- Poor organizational skills

1.3 The Consensus Conference

The Association on Dyslexia, in order to establish clinical standards for diagnosis on the rehabilitation of developmental dyslexia, promoted a Consensus Conference on DSA, that is, a meeting of professionals and lay people on dyslexia issues.

The main defining characteristic of this category is that of 'specificity,' understood as a disorder that affects a specific domain of ability in a significant but circumscribed way, leaving overall intellectual functioning intact.

In this sense, the main criterion necessary to establish the diagnosis of ASD is that of 'discrepancy' between ability in the specific domain affected (deficient relative to expectations for age and/or class attended) and general intelligence (appropriate for chronological age).

Two parameters were identified to define the discrepancy:

❖ Specific ability impairment must be less than minus two standard deviations of the expected values for age and class attended.

❖ The intellectual level must be in the normal range and not less than one standard deviation of the predicted values for the age and class attended, which is equivalent to an IQ of 85. From the definition of this concept derive some necessary indications to follow in order to have a correct diagnosis of ASD, such as the need to use standardized tests, both to measure general intelligence and specific ability; the exclusion of environmental situations of socio-cultural disadvantage that may interfere with appropriate instruction.

<u>Other useful criteria for defining ASD are:</u>

❖ the 'developmental' character of these disorders;

❖ the different expressiveness of the disorder in the various developmental stages of the skill in question;

❖ the almost constant association with other disorders (comorbidity), a fact that determines the marked heterogeneity of the functional and expressivity profiles with which ASD manifests themselves and that entails significant repercussions on the side of diagnostic investigation;

18

- ❖ the neurobiological character of the processual abnormalities that characterize ASD. It is equally important to emphasize that 'biological' factors actively interact in determining the onset of the disorder, with environmental factors;

- ❖ the specific disorder must result in a significant and negative impact on school adjustment and/ or activities of daily living.

However, it is important to emphasize that today the role of neurobiological factors is no longer a subject of debate and controversy, as it was in the past when some scholars attributed the origin of these disorders to psychogenic, pedagogical, or social factors.

In these criteria, reading fluency is recognized as a key aspect of characterizing dyslexia. To be focused on is the causal role of language factors in the genesis of the specific reading disorder.

1.4 False beliefs and strengths of DSA

Even today around debates on the topic of DSA, there are episodes of misinformation caused by stereotypes and prejudices. Most of them come precisely from those who are next to individuals with SLDs every day, i.e., parents, teachers, and pupils, while the remaining part spills over into the information that is conveyed to us by the new media. To such an extent that it was even possible to create a list in which the most widespread false beliefs were collected and reworked and listed below:

❖ DSA is a disease;

❖ People who have one or more DSA are not very smart because they cannot read and/or do the math;

❖ It is an effect of today's children's poor engagement in school;

❖ All DSA are dyslexic;

❖ Adolescents with DSA are lost;

❖ DSA is caused by poor teaching;

❖ Dyslexia is the effect of poor reading frequency;

❖ DSA in my time did not exist;

- ❖ DSA if they use a computer, text-to-speech and a calculator heal;

- ❖ Students with DSA are advantaged because they can use compensatory tools and dispensatory measures that oversimplify teaching and learning;

- ❖ Students with DSA will never learn a foreign language;

- ❖ Students with DSA if they perform a test correctly must have a lower grade than their peers for justice because it was shorter or easier;

- ❖ People with DSA are all geniuses;

- ❖ Kids with DSA are born without disorders and somehow get affected by them. These biases influence the perception that people with specific learning disorders learning have about themselves by generating a negative representation of their condition, medically termed 'Illness' and at the same time can influence the quality of social representation, medically termed 'Sickness'.

The greatest difficulties for people with specific learning disorders are found mostly in the world

21

of school, as the most severe time of the disorder coincides precisely with the school period where demands on the reading-writing level predominate. Yet these children are rich in strengths that often fail to emerge because they are stifled by the educational urgencies they must cope with in order not to fall behind the curriculum and the learning pace of their peers. The extensive reference literature agrees with the following strengths that are believed to be among the most common in students with ASD:

* intelligence;
* the ability to memorize pictures;
* an unusual and different approaches to school subjects;
* the ability to make unconventional connections;
* creativity and ability to easily produce new ideas;
* the propensity for selecting arguments in a discussion;
* skill in problem solving that requires imagining possible solutions;
* intuition and introspection;
* vivid imagination.

Teachers should enhance these characteristics, in a logic of educational personalization and individualization, even within the usual curricular activities focused mainly on skills in reading-writing and calculation.

The topic will be extensively taken up and dealt with specifically in the second chapter of the book.

1.5 Brief history of Dyslexia

One of the most important discoveries in human history has been the advent of reading and writing, a journey that started from far away and led the versatile human brain, in different ways, to adapt to the language code of reference in a given area of the world. Excluding the earliest attempts at writing by symbols by ancient prehistoric men, we can place the birth of writing around the fourth millennium B.C. with the advent of cuneiform writing by the Sumerians.

A 'further milestone in this journey is placed with the emergence of the first alphabets, such as at Ugarit in present-day Syria, and concludes in the eighth century B.C. with the perfection of the Greek alphabet. The latter was the first to present a precise correspondence between the phonemes of spoken Greek and the graphemes of the characters of the alphabet.

Thanks to Plato, who transcribed his master's oral dialogues, we know that Socrates criticized the advent of writing as guilty of targeting people's memory skills. Indeed, we read in the Phaedrus that according to Socrates words "will produce forgetfulness in the souls of those who learners, for lack of exercise of memory; precisely because, trusting in writing, they will remember things from without, from alien signs, and not from within, from themselves."

The first reports of people with inexplicable reading difficulties are revealed after the advent of the alphabet, and Plato himself speaks of intelligent people who inexplicably, despite exercises under guidance, could not learn the Greek alphabet correctly. Another case of reading difficulty was reported in the century A.D. by the Greek essayist Philostratus, who allegedly tried to help the son of Herod the Sophist, who had considerable difficulty learning the Greek alphabet.

Dyslexia, throughout human history, has always existed. One could trace a path of identification of four hypothetical stages, although not clearly differentiated, on the development of scientific theories on dyslexia: a first stage, the origins of dyslexia, in which the first subjects with reading and language deficits were identified, who were generally patients with acquired aphasia.

This period lasted until the end of the 19th century. During the first studies on developmental dyslexia (1895-1950), this condition was discovered and thus its causes and characteristics began to be analyzed. Later (1950-1970) there was a stage in which the field of dyslexia was opened to a variety of clinical, educational, and research approaches. Finally, modern theories (1970-2000) created the foundation of our current knowledge about dyslexia. The origins of dyslexia in the scientific literature are due to early findings of language problems, predominantly due to acquired aphasia.

These aphasic patients sometimes also suffered from a loss of reading ability. It took some major scientific discoveries before we were able to relate aphasia and dyslexia to brain lesions. It was in fact around the 16th century when philosophers and physicists decided that the location of thought was not the heart but the brain. Certainly, we must give credit to the work of Austrian doctor Franz Joseph Gall, who in the early 19th century suggested that each specific part of the brain has a specific function, and to that of Pierre Paul Broca, who located specific areas of the brain where language functions might reside. The term 'dyslexia' was first used in 1872 by German physician R. Berlin of Stuttgart, who used it to describe the case of an adult with acquired dyslexia, that is, the loss of reading ability due to brain injury.

Also in the same time frame, reading disorders were studied by German scientist Kussmaul, who defined them as disorders that generated 'word blindness.'

Similarly, Charcot defined 'alexia' as the total loss of the ability to read.

And finally Bateman, in 1890, defined 'alexia' or 'dyslexia' as a form of verbal amnesia in which the patient has lost memory of the conventional meaning of graphic symbols. Until that time, dyslexia was regarded as a disorder of neurological origin, thus caused by brain trauma (acquired dyslexia).

The term developmental dyslexia, on the other hand, was initially described as a visual disorder. In 1895 an article1 first came out in a scientific journal about a strange form of word blindness. It was written by an English surgeon, Hinshelwood who speculated that this condition was congenital and was less rare than it seemed based on the infrequency with which it was recorded.

This article inspired Dr. W. Pringle Morgan to describe the case of an intelligent fourteen-year-old boy who had not yet learned to read. For this Morgan is recognized as the father of developmental dyslexia.

In the 1920s, Orton was the first to introduce the term Developmental Dyslexia and raise awareness of the subject among the American public.

Until Orton's time, dyslexia was the exclusive field of physicians, especially ophthalmologists and neurologists. After Orton, dyslexia studies became an interesting field of analysis for psychologists, sociologists, and educators, who began to discuss the environmental and psychological factors that could be connected with the difficulties of dyslexia, such as educational methods and family life. Without going into the debate at that time about the causes and symptoms of dyslexia, however, there was a consensus among scholars that the disorder could be cured.

In the 1950s and 1960s, scholars began to support the hypothesis that dyslexia was a disorder with a multifactorial origin and thus began to recognize subgroups with visual, auditory, or abstract reasoning problems.

In France, Alfred Tomatis proposed that dyslexia was caused by an exclusively visual problem. Over time, subgroups with motor-type problems were discovered. It was not until the 1970s that a new hypothesis emerged that dyslexia originated from a deficit in the phonological system. Indeed, it was noted that dyslexics had difficulty recognizing that the words of the spoken language are formed by phonemes and associating these sounds with the corresponding alphabetical letters of the written language. After the 1970s, theories of dyslexia based on new disciplines, such as cognitive psychology and neuroscience, provided the most fascinating results.

In Italy at the level of public opinion, people began to talk about Dyslexia, mainly thanks to the autobiographical novel by journalist Ugo Pirro who told the story of his son. In the text emerges all the suffering of a father who understands the reason for the unexplained reading difficulties of his son, and the school suffering of his son, who only after years of guilt, learns that he is dyslexic, is presented.

The problem of dyslexia continues to linger and is still not solved. We continue to wonder what more is needed for us to understand that this disorder exists, it is not a disease, and it is not necessary to simply write the PDP (personal development planning) to circumvent the problem in the classroom.

CHAPTER 2

COPING WITH DYSLEXIA IN SCHOOL

D yslexia is a reading disorder that occurs in individuals of developmental age who lack neurological, cognitive, sensory, and relational deficits and who have enjoyed normal educational and schooling opportunities.

More specifically, dyslexia is the difficulty in controlling the written code, a difficulty that concerns the ability to read and write correctly and fluently.

Dyslexic children show ineffective automation of the reading process, a skill that should be structured by the third grade, the age at which the child should begin to speed up writing and, in reading access meaning directly.

Attention is focal, that is, the child focuses specifically

on decoding the text tiring quickly, making mistakes, falling behind, and consequently not learning.

Reading and writing should become automatic from third grade onward. Difficulty in reading can be more or less severe and is often accompanied by problems in writing, calculating, and sometimes in other mental activities; in fact, these three skills (reading writing, and arithmetic) have common bases.

In addition, a "subcategory" of developmental dyslexia concerns children with a previous Specific Language Disorder (Phonological Dyslexia).

Dyslexia is not caused by an intelligence deficit nor by environmental or psychological problems or by sensory or neurological deficits-on the contrary, they are intelligent and creative children.

School performance is often erratic leading teachers to believe that the child has difficulty with logic; in fact, the major difficulty is in deciphering the written code to make a reasoning.

Extensive studies show that the dyslexic child during reading has poor activation of brain mechanisms deputed to reading, which is matched by excessive activation of brain areas deputed to other activities.

It has also been shown how some skills such as linguistic, metalinguistic, visuospatial, etc are impaired only in their mutual functionality and not distinctly.

How dyslexia manifests itself?

The most recent research on the subject confirms the hypothesis of a constitutional origin of Developmental Dyslexia; that is, there would be a genetic and biological basis that originates the predisposition to the disorder.

Dyslexia tends, in fact, to be present in more than one member of the same family, although with different intensity.

Difficulties in reading and writing can be noticed as early as the last year of kindergarten (if exercises in pre-reading and pre-writing) or in first grade.

In developmental dyslexia what is diverted is the correctness and speed with which one reads; text comprehension is variable, generally good or sufficient.

Regarding reading correctness here are some of the typical errors:

1) Errors of visual type: exchange of letters that have similar or mirrored visual features ("e" with "a", "r" with

"e", "m" with "n", "b" with "d", "p" with "q" etc).

2) Phonological errors: exchange of letters that have the same "root" ("f" with "v", "c" with "g") etc.

Often the child with developmental dyslexia fails to learn multiplication tables and some sequential information such as the letters of the alphabet, days of the week, and months of the year; may get confused regarding spatial and temporal relationships (right/left; yesterday/Sunday; months and days) and may have difficulty verbally expressing what he thinks.

In some cases, there are difficulties in some motor skills, calculation, attention span, and concentration skills.

The child has difficulty copying from the blackboard and taking notes of orally given instructions. He sometimes loses self-confidence and may have behavioral alterations.

In fact, there are many undiagnosed dyslexic children who experience performance anxiety, depression, and low self-esteem.

The writing disorders associated with developmental dyslexia are called "Dysorthographies" i.e., difficulties in carrying out automatic text correction processes.

Errors are divided into:

1) Phonological errors

❖ Grapheme interchanges (b-p, b-d, f-v, r-l, p-q, a-e)

❖ omissions or additions of letters or syllables sp -> p: spoon -> poon

2) Non-phonological errors

❖ Illegal separations (in-group)

❖ Illegal mergers

❖ Homophonic grapheme interchange

3) Other errors

❖ Accents

❖ Doubles

Regarding learning style, it was found that in dyslexic children, the acquisition of skills related to the early stages of development (speaking, walking etc) was slower than average. In addition, their reading and writing ability is lower than intellectual liveliness; he has difficulty maintaining attention, finds it difficult to concentrate, and is very lively. He does well on oral exams but performs poorly on written ones.

The dyslexic child learns quickly through observation and especially through visual aids.

Regarding lateralization, he may have difficulty with tasks involving motor skills.

He has difficulty in synthesis and copying and in recognizing right from left.

In mathematics, he can only count on his fingers and is unable to learn algebra or calculus concepts.

Diagnosis

The diagnosis of developmental dyslexia must be both neuropsychological and global. It is important first to rule out, by objective means, sensory (of vision and hearing) neurological, cognitive, and emotional-relational deficits.

The disorder must be analyzed in its components in order to understand the child's areas of difficulty and especially the strategies he or she uses during reading; in fact, the child tends during the course of elementary school to implement compensatory strategies, that is, he or she tends to compensate with other skills for certain deficiencies.

It is essential that the diagnosis is the result of multidisciplinary work between neuropsychiatry, speech therapist, psychologist, psychopedagogist; in fact, the diagnosis must cover his cognitive abilities, praxis, and spatial skills, memory, language, and learning in the strict sense.

Here are just some of the most commonly used tests in clinical practice the following are indicated:

Attention:

- ❖ Stroop test
- ❖ Attentional matrices
- ❖ Digit-symbol
- ❖ Trail Making Test

Memory

- ❖ 15 Rey words
- ❖ Associated words
- ❖ Prose Memory
- ❖ Repetition of digits
- ❖ Tests of Courses

What to do after the diagnosis?

After diagnosis, if the child is in the first cycle of elementary school, speech therapy, focusing mainly on metaphonological skills, or neuropsychological therapy is generally recommended.

In the later stages, however, metacognitive intervention is recommended.

The environment, especially the family environment, must support the child, helping him or her in finding compensation strategies and especially in building a positive self-image.

It should first be made clear that dyslexics have a different way of learning, but they can learn.

What parents should do?

- ❖ Inform themselves about the problem

- ❖ Seek an appropriate diagnostic evaluation

- ❖ Discuss the problem with teachers

- ❖ Help him in school activities (read aloud to him)

- ❖ Supplement the reading with other information tools (USB, CD, video).

What the teacher must do?

- ❖ Really embrace "diversity," study it, communicate calmly with the child and show understanding

- ❖ Talk to the class and not hide the problem (one way is to ask each child in the class to expose one of their difficulties to their classmates)

- ❖ Explain to the class why dyslexics are treated differently on various occasions

- ❖ Utilize the resources of classmates by, for example, assigning a Tutor to the dyslexic child

- ❖ Actively collaborate with peers

- ❖ Continuously communicate with parents

- ❖ Communicate and interact with health services

- ❖ Know the stages of writing and reading acquisitions and know how to conduct phonological and metaphonological work

- ❖ Regarding elementary, middle, and high school:

recognize the types of spelling errors, know how to take stock of reading in one's classroom, do metacognitive work on reading, work on study skills, and Evaluate taking into account starting points. These last caveats will be taken up at the end of the book in a specific chapter.

CHAPTER 3

CREATIVE GENIUS IN DYSLEXICS

3.1 The personality of the dyslexic

Having dyslexia will not make every dyslexic a genius, but it will benefit his or her self-esteem to know that one's mind, functions exactly like that of great geniuses. Not all dyslexics develop the same gifts, but all have common characteristics.

A list could be compiled with what are called the core abilities shared by all dyslexics:

1. They are able to use their ability to alter and create perceptions (primary ability).
2. They are acutely aware of their surroundings.
3. They are more curious than average.
4. They think mainly in pictures rather than words.
5. They have a lot of insight and introspection.
6. They think and perceive multi-dimensionally (using all the senses).

7. They can feel their thinking as real.

8. They have vivid imaginations.

These abilities generally, if not suppressed by parents or school, will be able to be translated into two characteristics, such as above-average intelligence and creative abilities.

In general, characterizing the personality of a dyslexic person are the following aspects:

1. Appears lively, of vivid intelligence but unable to read and write or speak at a certain level.

2. Described as lazy, taciturn, inattentive, immature, not trying hard enough, may have behavior problems.

3. Often has a high IQ, and shows success in school in oral subjects but not in writing.

4. Appears taciturn, has low self-esteem; hides and conceals weaknesses with ingenious compensation strategies. Easily frustrated and emotional about literature and school tests.

5. Skilled in art and drama, music, sports, mechanical things, storytelling, sales, commerce, drawing, construction, and engineering.

6. Has the air of a crackpot or often a daydreamer; can easily lose track of time.

7. Hardly holds attention for a prolonged time.

In writing and motor skills, he also:

1. Problems in writing; handwriting is variable or illegible.

2. Clumsy, uncoordinated. Mediocre in dancing or team games, and has difficulty in motor skills.

3. May be ambidextrous and often confuses the spatial concepts of left-right, above-below.

In math and time management (organization):

1. Has difficulty in talking about time, managing it, learning information and tasks in succession, or being on time.

2. In doing the math he shows a dependence on counting on his fingers and other stratagems, knows the answers, but cannot execute them on paper.

3. Can count but has difficulty counting objects and dealing with money.

4. Can do arithmetic but fails at problems, does not master algebra or higher mathematics.

5. Learns best through hands on, experience, demonstration, experimentation, observation, and visual aids.

In vision, reading, and spelling:

1. While reading complains of dizziness, headache, or stomachache.

2. Is confused by letters, numbers, words, sequences, or explanations.

3. When reading or writing makes repetitions,

additions, transpositions, omissions, substitutions, and reversals of letters, numbers, and/or words.

4. Seems to have difficulty with vision, yet eye exams reveal no problems.

5. From extremely keen eyesight he is gifted with powers of observation, depth perception, and peripheral vision.

6. Reads and rereads with little comprehension.

7. Reads phoneme by phoneme inconsistently.

In hearing and speech:

1. Has expanded hearing, hears things unspoken or apparent to others, and is easily distracted by sounds.

2. Has difficulty translating thoughts into words, speaks in hesitant sentences, leaves sentences unfinished, stutters when under stress, mispronounces long words, or transposes sentences, words and syllables when speaking.

In memory and perception:

1. Has excellent long-term memory of experiences, places, and faces.

2. Poor memory for sequences, facts, and news he has not experienced.

3. Thinks mainly with images and feeling, not with sounds or words (little inner dialogue).

In behavior, health, development, and personality:

1. Extremely disordered or coercively ordered.

1 1 0   1   1 0 0 1 1 1 1 0 0 1 1   1 1 1 0 0 1 1 0
0 0 1
1 0 0
0 0
1 1 0
1   0
1
1   1
0 1 1
0
1 0 1
0 0 0
1 1 1
1 0
1 1
0 1
1

2. May be the class clown, troublemaker, or, conversely, too calm.

3. Prone to ear infections, sensitive to foods, additives, and chemicals.

4. May be an exceptional sleeper, deep or light sleeper, possible to urinate in bed beyond the appropriate age.

5. Has a strong sense of justice; emotionally sensitive strives for perfection.

6. Errors and symptoms increase dramatically with confusion, time pressure, emotional stress, and poor health.

0

3.2 Mind strengths and weaknesses.

I became aware of the work of Mr. and Mrs. Eide entitled The Dyslexic Advantage, from which you can either view a video directly from the blog or read it in e-book. It is important to realize that one in five people is dyslexic and that for every pupil identified as such, three will not be. Mr. and Mrs. Eide specifically address the advantages of being dyslexic (The Dyslexic Advantage Unlocking the Hidden Potential of the Dyslexic Brain) identifying several strengths: Material, Interconnected, Narrative, and Dynamic. In one word: MIND. They begin to explain them with this metaphor:

'Imagine that you have always lived on a remote island, where you have never been able to have contact with anyone and where no artifacts from the outside world have ever arrived.

One day while walking on the beach you spot a cylindrical tube hidden in the sand of the beach. You pick it up, clean it, and with extreme excitement, you realize that you have found a human artifact, but you cannot figure out what it really is.

On further analysis, you discover that at the ends of the

cylinder are two lenses, one of which is twice the size of the other, and that sunlight reflects off them. You inspect the mystery object again and guess that light is passing through it. You then bring your eye closer to the larger lens and realize that looking through the cylinder you see a wonderful miniature of the world around you. You thus think you understand the use of that mysterious object: it is used to see the world around--shrunken down!

Actually, it is, but it is not!

A telescope shrinks images if you look at them from one end, but enlarges them if you look at them from the opposite end. Like a telescope, the concept of dyslexia is a human invention and like a telescope, it can either stretch and clarify our view of those individuals who struggle to read and write correctly, or, used in reverse, it can narrow our view of those individuals.

Unfortunately, this 'narrowing' effect is precisely what, we believe, has happened to the way the concept of dyslexia is used. Turning to examine them individually, the first one we talk about is the M or material strength, the one that primarily aids reasoning in both the physical and material world, in relation to the shape, size, position, or orientation of objects in space and the way they interact. These individuals have a global vision that enables them to imagine, dynamically, how a process will develop over time. The spatial ability that can be extraordinarily useful in school.

However, people with this ability receive little attention and these skills are not enhanced. The other side of the coin highlights the dark side of strength M, namely the relative weakness in certain 2D processing skills. The one area in which dyslexics might experience major problems is symbol reversal during reading or writing. Another disadvantage noted, in this strength, is a language difficulty. Parents and teachers are often puzzled to discover that these students freeze when faced with seemingly simple answers, especially in writing and if the time given to them is short.

The second strength is the 'interconnected, I, whose basic skills are three:

1. The ability to identify relationships between different objects of thought. The relationships are of two types: similarities and associations. Similarities can link ideas, and concepts but also feelings, emotions, or information of any kind and can range from literal to figurative similarities.

Several research studies support the idea that dyslexic people, as a group, show particular talents for finding similarities and likenesses.

2. The ability to shift perspectives and approaches, which gives the ability to see that a particular problem, idea, or phenomenon can be studied using different approaches and techniques borrowed from different disciplines or professions. Those who possess it prefer interdisciplinarity to specialized approaches when they have to tackle new problems or projects. What dyslexics with this trait manage to do is get to the substance rather than the detail; it makes them adept at understanding a text where passages provide useful background contexts, even when reading is slow, due in large part to their ability to use contextual clues.

3. The ability to reason with a global perspective, which reflects the faculty to perceive the whole and how the parts relate to each other. For this reason, instead of sorting things into categories, they combine them together. They are very aware of the personal relationships between people and how things pass from one to another.

One of the reasons concerning the employment of more than 100 dyslexic or dyspraxic intelligence officers, in the British services team, GCHQ3, is perhaps this. In fact, the conductor of the dyslexic and dyspraxic support group here said that people with neurobiological diversity, have remarkable investigative skills, fitting the profile of an agent Government Communication Head Quarter, Government Communications Headquarters, which is located in Cheltenham (Headquarters), UK, and is the government agency responsible for security, as well as espionage and counter-espionage, in the communications area, an activity technically known as SIGINT (SIGnal INTelligence).

Secret, meaning that in some cognitive areas the capabilities are average, while in others they have superior ones. The concept is seemingly difficult to understand.

Returning to strengths, the narrative ones, N, represent the ability to construct a connected series of mental scenes from fragments of a past personal experience, which can be used to recall the past, explain the present, simulate a potential future or imaginary scenarios, and understand and test important concepts. They derive their power from a kind of memory known as episodic or personal memory, which allows the acquisition or retrieval of information related to specific events located in time, enabling the accurate recording of experience with precise autobiographical reference. These people have the ability to learn from experience, with a tendency to store conceptual and verbal knowledge as representations or examples rather than abstract verbal definitions. For example, if we wanted to ask a dyslexic person to give us a definition of << bicycle >>, he or she would be likely to respond with an analogy: "it is like a motorcycle, but you have to pedal it," or "it is a thing with a seat, two wheels, a handlebar, two pedals, and you go by pushing the pedals with your feet," instead of responding with an abstract description, such as "it is a two-wheeled means of transportation."

This reliance on fact-based representations rather than abstract or noncontextual concepts reflects a greater reliance on episodic memory than on semantic memory, that is, a memory that has lost its spatiotemporal coordinates. This style of creative narrative thinking often shows a tendency to think and communicate information in story form.

Also in the reference text, The Dyslexic Advantage, several studies report that many dyslexic individuals resort to this type of storytelling and their descriptions often contain elements such as analogies, metaphors, and personalization.

The last strength, analyzed by Mr. and Mrs. Eide, is what is referred to as dynamic reasoning, D. It is closely related to narrative reasoning in that it is the ability to reason in dynamic contexts, that is when information is incomplete or varies over time. People skilled in this ability often work in business, financial markets, in scientific fields to reconstruct past events such as geologists or paleontologists. The weakness is given by 'having poor efficiency since their approach is intuitive, they fail to create a mental sequence of the process, and thus, to explain the various steps.

3.3 Visual-spatial skills.

Included among the functional characteristics and particularly developed in individuals with dyslexia are what have been termed visuospatial skills. This, like other qualities identified in dyslexics, was addressed by one who knew quite a bit about dyslexia, Thomas West.

A dyslexic and author of the book The Mind's Eye, he began his research on dyslexia when he realized that his own children were also dyslexic; he currently gives seminars around the world, where he exhibits the research programs he conducts on visualization. As I mentioned earlier, according to West, dyslexics have a more visual way of thinking, that is, they proceed by associations of images and show a more global approach to problems with particular abilities in understanding complex systems in economic affairs and the sciences. It is as if to compensate, they are able to enhance other characteristics. He still claims that dyslexics have excellent visualization power, including visualization in three dimensions.

Visual literacy is the basis of new technologies. Dyslexics have extreme difficulty in reading, but if the same is organized in a different system, which can be a figure, a map, or another form of visualization, everything can change. The dyslexic uses thought forms in which images are generated or called to mind and manipulated, covered, translated, or associated with other similar forms. This can be applied to new technologies that exploit the ability of thought to speak in images.

For dyslexics, visual literacy is an easier approach because it is more immediate. It is as if the new technologies exhume the primal abilities of the brain; as when primitive man had to interpret the signs of nature to survive.

But to what extent can visuospatial ability be important in space-time organization and in the process of writing and reading?

The activities of reading and writing become possible when the child can orient himself in the space adjacent to it and is able to understand the temporal relationships between elements.

Reading, then, involves the transformative capacities of thinking, those that enable operations on data, which underlie any symbolic and abstract cognitive project.

Operations on data are, for example, the ability to make comparisons between signs to establish equality and diversity, to anticipate with eye movement the program of sound emission, and to take into account objective references (the paper, the margins) and relate them to oneself. This could lead to the claim that dyslexia and dysgraphia are a dysfunction in the ability to operate on data according to the parameters of space and time.

Often dyslexia has upstream a disturbance in body schema knowledge, understood as spatial self-knowledge, as a proprioceptive schema endowed with left-right symmetry. We are talking about children who are regularly active in moving, as motor skills are intact, but unable to reflect on their movements, unaware, for whom movement is acted upon, but not represented in the mind as taking place in space, with a direction, a shape, a direction. It is the ill-defined lateralization that generates spatial disorientation and has considerable correlations with dyslexia.

Visual-spatial skills are by far the most important, essential prerequisite for all future student learning. These refer to the ability to integrate information from perceptual space, to use and organize it to adequately perform different tasks. A child with poor visuospatial skills, even if perfectly gifted from a verbal point of view, will present difficulties in all school subjects. With significant frequency, dyslexia is accompanied by disorders of lateralization and space-time organization. The acquisition of the body schema, in relation to space, presents deficiencies in order to the correct distinction between left and right side, the perception of orientation in the concepts of "front-back', "high-low', with impediments to maintaining regular and constant dynamics of gaze movement during reading and consequent inability to analyze and synthesize complex visual stimuli such as words (the dyslexic frequently changes the direction of gaze, moving now from right to left, now correctly from left to right, now from bottom to top, now from top to bottom, without following the succession of elements imposed by the text, but arbitrarily skipping lines and words).

When the epicenter of perception is shifted, this causes disorientation, where precisely a person's perceptions become distorted. The most important senses that are altered are vision, hearing, balance, movement, and time. During disorientation, the brain sees things moving that are not actually moving; it causes the altered perceptions, to be accepted as real. Everyone experiences disorientation at times, but for the dyslexics this is a feeling they have pushed far beyond the ordinary. Dyslexics do not merely experience it, but cause it without realizing it, to have multi-dimensional perceptions. They also use it to become more perceptual or imaginative than average, for creative imagination. Dyslexics need to form mental images that they can use and with which they can think by associating these visual and auditory images with the words they are trying to learn.

When they have to communicate their thoughts, they first have to catch precise images in their head and then put them in order so that they can memorize them. Then they have to find the words to describe their pictures and then they have to find the pictures so that they can speak. Because they see the letters as drawings, they cannot read the symbol, suffering the interruption of what should have been a natural process of transition from image to symbol, thus not using their resources.

Very important in this regard is the explanation of the stages of the disorientation mechanism:

1. The child is not interested in what the teacher is saying because he is using only words and not pictures;

2. Boredom and confusion activate the perceptual alteration function of the brain;

3. The child becomes disoriented;

4. While bored, confused and disoriented his internal clock speeds up and so time seems to slow down;

5. The child's senses are distorted, including the sense of balance and movement;

6. if he stands still he will have the sensation of moving, to the point of being seasick;

7. conversely, if he starts moving, the sensations will be reversed and he will feel as if he is still;

8. To compensate for the seasickness situation and to stop the nausea he will continue to move;

The situation precipitates when the teacher asks him to behave differently, i.e., to sit still at the mercy of seasickness and simultaneously follow the lesson better.

The appearance of disorientation can also be related to the concept of trigger words, those that have abstract meanings, and often a large number of different meanings. For the most part, they are adjectives, articles, adverbial locutions, pronouns, verbs, etc. They confuse dyslexics since they do not represent concrete objects or actions. The disorientation can lead to dyslexics appearing clumsy. In particular, one type of chronic clumsiness that dyslexics suffer from is called dyspraxia. It is not always associated with dyslexia because it does not directly affect reading, writing, spelling, or math. It is one of the many facets of the gift of dyslexia. Dyspraxia causes the senses of balance and movement to be distorted because of disorientation, an obvious fact since dizziness is always caused by disorientation.

Returning to the concept of visuospatial ability...

Two British researchers, Parkinson and Edwards, have also shown that the visuospatial categories in which dyslexics exhibit the greatest qualities are two:

1. Intelligence/awareness/management of shapes and space in three dimensions;
2. Intelligence/awareness/management of complex work in an innovative way.

The hypothesis these researchers propose is based on the difference between cognitive processes involved with the one-dimensional aspects of language and the three-dimensional aspects of vision. They believe that the nature of this difference may be responsible for the difficulties, language-related, in dyslexics, but also for their talent.

Dr. Linda Silverman (director of the Institute for the Study of Advanced and Gifted Development Center. Colorado) was the first to identify the concept of Visual- Spatial Learners, that is, people who learn Visuospatially. Silverman claims that all the people she examined had a parent who exhibited this way of learning, so she is of the opinion that this learning style is hereditary.

3.4 Creative genius

What sets humanity above other living forms is creativity. Particularly in dyslexics, the creative need is stronger than in individuals who lack their own basic abilities. For these individuals, creativity is most pronounced through thinking in images, intuitive thinking, and curiosity. All original ideas come from the creative process.

At a very basic level, it is the means by which true learning takes place. The word itself evokes genius and originality; in everyday life, it is an indispensable condition of existence, and everything that has something new in it owes its origin to the creative process.

It could also be defined as an essential component of mental life, present in all people, albeit in different measures.

For one to speak of creativity there must be the production of something (an artifact or idea) that did not exist before, to which other people attribute meaning and which turns out to have some utility or is of some importance. New, meaningful, and interesting certainly when we talk about creativity, it comes naturally to mind the production of something extraordinary or revolutionary, so much so that we are inclined to regard it as a skill belonging only to great geniuses or artists. But this type of creativity is only one of two that can be distinguished: it is what is called big-C, great creativity. The other type, small-C, small creativity, is that the creative process not involving radical transformations, but simple changes that can lead to improvement.

We are thus talking about a component of mental life that is present in everyone, albeit in different measures, and that can be stimulated.

Three basic mechanisms recur in the creative process:

1. Widening of perspective: it is important to move in a vast mental field with which it is possible to take in ideas, leading us to think of new innovations, and to produce something novel and original. The U.S. psychologist Guilford, in 1960, introduced the distinction between two styles of thinking: convergent thinking, used in well-defined contexts and when situations allow a single correct response; divergent thinking, in situations where the ways out are varied, producing something new. It is in divergent thinking that creative thinking would be identified, which has characteristics such as fluidity

(ability to produce many ideas without reference to their appropriateness), flexibility (ability to think easily from one category of elements to another in the course of the flow of thought), originality (ability to come up with unusual or unique ideas to which other people do not converge).

2. The connection of different elements into a creative product: creative processes are composed of connections, usually consisting of an association of elements that we believe have nothing in common with each other or a combination of elements in an unusual way. For an individual to produce creative associations, two factors must occur, namely, the abundance of ideas arising in his or her mind and the subject's ease in moving to the lower levels of the hierarchy of elements associated with a concept

3. Reorganization of patterns of interpretation: insight (intuition) is the appropriate response that distinguishes the creative process. The subject has a kind of illumination, by which the situation suddenly presents itself to him in a new light. In order to perform a creative act, a process, accommodation, takes place, which modifies a mental schema to make it adequate to understand a situation that it fails to account for. One must overthrow habitual mental patterns to be creative.

Maslow sees creativity as fundamental among the innate needs of humans and a factor in personal well-being, as it provides a positive view of self.

Creativity is developed through the creative process, which consists of the following important and fundamental characteristics:

- ❖ Constancy: 'genius is in holding on...genius is 1% inspiration and 99% sweat';

- ❖ Time: fundamental in a society like today's culture of haste, where one must set oneself unlimited time to be an explorer;

- ❖ Ability to concentrate: great achievements of ingenuity are possible only if an individual is able to concentrate for a long time on a single goal, free from distractions and not conditioned by other concerns. It is therefore necessary to set oneself up in a space of one's own that provides privacy and isolation, as well as a detachment from others;

- ❖ Practice: tantamount to continually testing one's abilities, acts necessary for the realization of creative potential;

- ❖ Ability to ask questions: as George Bernard Shaw said: "The questions that are most difficult to answer, are those whose answer is obvious";

- ❖ Selective combination: being able, once you have found the indispensable information, to be able to creatively connect it, and associate it;

- ❖ Transfer: the stimulating of finding an appropriate adaptation of the creative idea and discovering patterns or relationships;

❖ Error, frustration, despair: these have also been accepted by dyslexics themselves as necessary stages to go through in the creative process;

❖ Plot of endeavors: if the stage of frustration has been reached in the project, it can be put aside momentarily and devoted to something else;

❖ Childlike freshness: the creative spirit does not decline with age, but gains strength and vigor as a person begins to focus more on what really matters in life. Creativity also feeds on the initial efforts of children's early symbolic products;

❖ Imagination: creativity can be understood as applied imagination; to create something new, to think up new problems and questions, one must employ one's imagination; it is influenced by the structures of cognition, a phenomenon known in psychology as structured imagination, which shows that even the most innovative ideas contain something old;

The creative process often results in a dynamic oscillation between opposites: for any inventor to know the relationship between opposites often leads to a creative solution.

Some scholars of creativity have tried to understand the creative process by breaking it down into different stages. The best-known description of the creative process is by successive stages proposed by English psychologist and educator Graham Wallas with Richard Smith, authors of the text The art of thought published in 1926.

There are five stages described, but in most publications, they are reduced to four:

1. Preparation: the gathering of materials and information to work on and their organization. It calls for a methodical and systematic attitude. Sometimes an investigation is set in motion by a stroke of luck. Characteristics of this stage seem to be: the ability to identify a problem, familiarity with basic facts, and orientation toward finding a solution.

2. Incubation: the mental processing of available materials in search of an order that produces new meaning. It is a process that develops by trial and error seemingly disordered, seesaw streams of thought. It continues even at times when conscious attention is suspended. Einstein began at age 16 to worry about certain fundamental problems in physics related to the meaning of the speed of light. When he realized that the problem could be solved by questioning the concept of time, it took him only five weeks to draft his famous theory of relativity, even though he was working full-time at the Swiss patent office.

3. Enlightenment or insight: the often instantaneous

intuition of the existence of an unexpected solution that is different from anything previously assumed. It seems to occur spontaneously and unexpectedly, often combined with a strong emotional reaction.

4. Verification: testing, fine-tuning, and formalization. The scientific method requires that discovery is presented through formal argumentation, starting with a set of axioms or fundamental principles. Structuring an intuition in the terms of a formal argument becomes a way of verifying its consistency. Einstein said: "It is very rare that I think in words. The thought flashes through my mind, and only later can I try to express it...all these years I have had the feeling that I am moving in a definite direction, toward something concrete...something profoundly different from later considerations of the logical form of the solution." Of course behind this sense of a definite direction, there is always something logical; but for me, it always presents itself as a kind of general look; in a sense, visually.

The missing phase, which Wallas calls intimation and is predominantly presented as a sub-phase, is the feeling of being on the right track, accompanied by rising excitement, which sometimes precedes insight.

The sequence proposed by Wallas is plausible and involves alternating between logical and analogical thinking. Logical thinking proceeds linearly, by sequences (cause/effect, before/after, premises/consequences), while analogical thinking proceeds nonlinearly by similarities/differences, suggestions, and metaphors.

They require logical and structured reasoning in the first stage, and the last. They require analogical thinking in the second stage and the third.

Osborn, on the other hand, divided the creative process into seven stages, using different terminology:

1. Orientation: focusing on the problem.
2. Preparation: gathering relevant data.
3. Analysis: breaking down the relevant material.
4. Ideation: accumulating alternatives in the form of ideas.
5. Incubation: 'resting,' to encourage enlightenment.
6. Synthesis: putting the pieces together.
7. Evaluation: judging the resulting ideas.

From the various subdivisions and diagrams, which illustrate the creative process broken down into stages, a clear operational methodology of creativity emerges, a path in which analysis (corresponding to the stages of preparation and verification) is intertwined with synthesis (which occurs at the time of incubation and illumination).

Also of interest becomes the process regarding the stimulation of creativity, where important are keeping our creative muscle exercised, and keeping the brain active, a factor that involves our feeling good since when we activate it to learn something new, it releases dopamine into our system, i.e., a neurotransmitter that makes us feel serene; being distracted, a condition in which we develop new ideas and solutions to a possible problem, leaving the brain at rest, in a condition of total freedom and leisure; getting out of the everyday environment, experimenting with new ideas and methods of work helps us to see things from a new perspective; returning to being a beginner to have many more possibilities, than in the mind of an expert.

Creativity may appear to be an innate characteristic that is difficult to have. In reality, it just needs to be stimulated and trained every day. It becomes necessary in any case to make the environment in which one works, stimulating.

110 1 1001111001 1 1111 00110
0 0 1
1 0 0
0 0
1 1 0
1   0
  1
1   1
0 1 1
    0
1 0 1
0 0 0
1 1 1
1 0
1 1
0 1
  1

3.5 Distinguished dyslexic geniuses

What do Albert Einstein, George Clooney, Napoleon Bonaparte, and Vincent Van Gogh have in common? Their dyslexia, or rather the tenacity with which they managed to overcome the difficulties associated with this learning disorder, brought out their creative potential.

The scientific literature on dyslexia has for years been collecting and disseminating the stories of famous people who were or are dyslexic.

This is to make it clear that the situation of educational disadvantage experienced by individuals with DSA, will not imply in the future their failure or not being able to develop life projects or areas. It is through the tenacity that is employed that talent, a small but important part, comes out.

If we wanted, first of all, to identify what is generally expressed by the term genius, it would come naturally to refer to a person with an unusually high score on the IQ test, or an extraordinarily collective person. Mark Twain states, 'He who is truly great makes you feel that you too can become great,' or again Michelangelo:

'Genius is to have unremitting patience.'

In the majority of documented cases of famous dyslexics, figures from the Anglo-Saxon world stand out in a particular way because, pertaining to the field of dyslexia studies, they appear to be more gifted. Moreover, some of them were artists in multiple fields, such as Francis Bacon (philosopher, politician, scientist) or multifaceted personalities such as Leonardo Da Vinci, Michelangelo Buonarroti, Alexander Bell.

It is not easy to attribute a diagnosis of dyslexia to each one, but from their biographies, it can be assumed that they had a disorder related to reading, writing, and math.

Many of these characters have epilepsy in common: Julius Caesar, Michelangelo, Napoleon. Van Gogh, who suffered from several disorders, stands out. In particular, the following episode gives pause for thought: in the last period of his life, it is known that the author, in a moment of madness, amputated his left ear. Well, in the self-portrait he later painted, the right ear is seen bandaged instead of the left, hinting at a characteristic typical of some dyslexics, which is the difficulty of lateralization.

Scarce in the list seem to be the names of female characters, not due to a factor related to sex, chromosomes, or genes or the fact that dyslexia is more present in the male sex, but because regarding the past we know that children rarely studied and that only noblewomen had a tutor.

Recent characters are the writer Agatha Christie, and the first lady Anna Eleanor Roosevelt.

Unhappy accounts from the lives of dyslexic geniuses should give pause for thought; here are some examples:

- ❖ Albert Einstein's teacher described him as mentally slow, unsociable, and lost in his absurd dreams, and later, his Greek teacher told him he would never be anyone.

- ❖ Louis Pasteur was rated as mediocre in chemistry when he attended the Royal College.

- ❖ Ludwig Van Beethoven had a music teacher who told him that as a composer he was hopeless.

- ❖ George Washington's brother suggested that perhaps the most appropriate job for him was forestry inspector.

❖ A newspaper editor fired Walt Disney because he lacked imagination and did not have good ideas.

In conclusion, dyslexic geniuses can be described as particularly special people because they overcame or circumvented the obstacles they encountered, realizing their dreams and desires. Moreover, it is possible to identify many artistic fields or fields characterized by high levels of creativity and ingenuity, outstanding people, or forms with a difficult school experience due to their learning disorders. Not all dyslexics have out-of-the-ordinary talents, but they certainly present strengths that they should also find in the world of schooling.

3.6 The correlation between dyslexia and creativity

Dyslexia, in some cases, contributes to success in the creative field. Although dyslexics have limitations in reading and writing, they have a marked ability to use lateral thinking, and creativity, that is commanded by the right hemisphere.

In this regard, some researchers have hypothesized that individuals who are particularly gifted in certain areas, sometimes at the expense of other abilities, as in the case of dyslexics, have altered brain lateralization. Both language disorders and lack of right lateralization of motor functions are therefore believed to be indicative of altered brain lateralization, as studies using PET brain visualization techniques suggest.

Scientists at McMaster University in Ontario, Canada, led by Dr. Sandra Witelson, analyzed Einstein's brain, preserved after his death, finding peculiarities in the parietal region, which specializes in perception three-dimensional and mathematics. These formed differently and are the largest the researchers have ever seen, each hemisphere of Einstein's brain is 15 percent larger and weighs about 12 percent more, with a thinner cerebral cortex than normal. From this example, one can draw in conclusion about how each brain is different in every facet and how each is associated with talent, an event that even scientists cannot explain why.

Several hypotheses have emerged from more recent studies regarding the association between dyslexia and creativity:

1. It can be accepted as real and based on a specific neurological process arising from the original

processing related to dyslexia.

2. It may be related to general comorbidity, where a generally unknown factor, generated both dyslexia and creativity, with no connection between the two.

3. May reflect compensation for failures in school skills.

4. May depend on the activation of original strategies and unconventional ways of thinking due to frustrations resulting from reading and writing problems. Therefore, creativity and artistic inclination may be the unexpected effect of such frustrations.

5. May be an illusion based on the obvious discrepancy between reading achievement and artistic talent.

The reason for the success of creative people is the ability to work hard.

The fundamental concept is fact that education and creativity should proceed in the same direction. Parents and educators should understand that the talents and special abilities displayed by each of them are quite different from the talents and abilities that are highly regarded in a conventional academic setting, especially in the early school years.

What matters and is important to keep in mind in order to develop talents and not stifle them, is not to use the child's interests to punish or bribe them by making promises; not to forget that we are still children in front of us and as such they have the same hopes and needs as any other human being; to think outside the box; to avoid chaos and competition; to recognize success and not the winner, and to understand that this child's development will never follow a predictable and homogeneous path.

Gifted dyslexic children are referred to in the English language as twice exceptional, meaning twice extraordinary, as are other gifted children who have other disabilities.

The creative abilities, intellectual effort, and passion they put into their hobbies are clear indicators of their potential gifts. It is clear that sometimes they are so frustrated that they use their creative ability to avoid work. Because of this, they may develop low self-esteem; some of them, feeling constantly challenged, and exposed to constant failure, may incur states of anxiety and depression.

This is what is told in the film Stars on Earth as the Solomon Islands anecdote: here when the people of a tribe want to deforest a piece of the jungle, to make the land for cultivation, they don't cut down the trees, but they approach the tree and begin to insult it, stubbornly, then curse it. The tree eventually, dries up and then falls to the ground without any need to cut it down.

Anxiety, frustration, and resentment can, therefore, affect conduct, disturbing social relations.

110 1 100111100111 1111 00110
001
100
0 0
110
1 0
1
101
011
0
101
000
111
10
11
01
1

CHAPTER 4

DYSLEXIA AS TOLD BY A DYSLEXIC

4.1 The story of Ronald D. Davis.

Born profoundly autistic and in school considered mentally retarded, it took a full thirty-eight years for Ronald Davis (born 1942) to believe he was a complete human being. The abuse he suffered at home, the humiliation at school, despite the fact that at the age of seventeen his IQ had been tested at one hundred and thirty-seven, to emerge from the terrible diagnosis of " Kenner syndrome" which meant he would never be able to be touched, to learn, to speak or to achieve much more than a chimpanzee could be the figure of his mother who unlike his father and siblings became his greatest supporter.

The speech therapist's work meant that he began to speak fluently at the age of nineteen, although he could not yet read, as he was prevented by dyslexia.

Until the age of thirty-eight, while continuing to hide his non-illiteracy, he established himself as a famous engineer, inventor, and businessman.

What profoundly changed his experience and understanding of reality was an experiment performed on his own perceptions in 1981, which enabled him to correct and control involuntary perceptual distortions, the basis of his dyslexia. For the first time in his life, he was able to read a book, from beginning to end, effortlessly.

In 1982, together with a school psychologist, Dr. Fatima Ali, he pioneered an intensive, week-long counseling program to correct dyslexia in adults and children, thus opening the doors to the Reading

Research Council in Burlingame, California. Since then he has dedicated his life to helping people with the gift of dyslexia by boosting their self-esteem and correcting their literacy. His methods, known as Davis Dyslexia Correction, are changing the face of special education and treatment for these difficulties around the world. The unique aspect of his work consists of a series of perceptual and kinaesthetic exercises, called Davis Orientation Counseling, which teaches dyslexic students to recognize and control the mental state that leads them to the disorientation and confusion produced by letters, words, and numbers.

Important are the Davis Symbol Mastery or creative learning procedures and reading exercises, which enable dyslexic students to learn to read.

In 1994 he developed his paper The Gift of Dyslexia, published in response to the continuing demand from parents and educators for a detailed book, containing specifically, the methods of correction he devised. The book that in the spring of 1995 was published in English, French, German, Dutch, and Spanish, reaching as many as 18 languages to date.

Also in 1995, together with his wife Alice, he founded

the Davis Dyslexia Association International (DDAI). The goals promulgated are to raise awareness, worldwide, of the positive aspects of dyslexia and related difficulties in learning and to present methods to improve literacy.

4.2 The Gift of Dyslexia and the Davis Method.

As mentioned above, one of Ronald Davis' writings, is the text The Gift of Dyslexia. Tracing a linear path of the salient features of dyslexia, Davis arrives at the conclusion that through the gift of creativity, he was able to develop and implement a revolutionary new method to correct this disorder, along with general learning disorders. He derives an evolutionary theory from it and proposes concrete acts and behaviors explained to parents, teachers, therapists, and the dyslexics themselves.

The font intentionally used for writing the text stands out immediately, that is, larger than normal and with as few punctuation marks as possible, so as to be more understandable to the dyslexic.

It is as if he wanted to make the experience real as if he wanted to provide us with the introspection needed to teach effectively.

Davis provides keys in the opening to better interpret his work, such as understanding that the dyslexic's learning style is actually to be understood as a talent; understanding the dimensional awareness in which he lives; conceptualizing disorientation, and finally techniques for controlling this as well as the general symptoms he experiences.

Orientation, disorientation, and mastery, are terms we find frequently in the text. By educators and psychologists, Davis' concept of orientation, is recognized as attention and would lead to preventing both disorientation and confusion, which arise from working with symbols for reading, writing, spelling, calculating, and achieving greater visual stability, attention, and feeling of control.

The Symbol Mastery Techniques developed by Davis are used to improve a student's writing and reading skills, harnessing every sense to teach and provide integration of concepts as students touch, see, hear, discuss, and theorize about the information they are learning.

Long-term learning arises precisely from these procedures, from a multisensory application that provides stimulation of important parts of the brain. One should not overlook the clear difference between attention and concentration, seemingly similar terms, but separating them is a gulf. For a dyslexic child, paying attention is almost natural and easy, but concentrating becomes difficult. When someone pays attention, his or her awareness is widespread, covering the entire surroundings. When one is focused, most or one's attention is fixed on one thing in the immediate surrounding environment. Davis states that, according to him, intense concentration produces a kind of mnemonic learning, where there is memorization but not comprehension, leading children to go through several steps without fully grasping the concepts underlying the topics taught.

To overcome disorientation, which I have discussed at length above, Davis provides us with simple procedures such as the 'Davis Orientation Protocol' and 'Symbol Mastery.' The dyslexia correction process adopted by Davis always includes both.

Dyslexics need to form mental images that they can use and with which they can think and associate with the words they are trying to learn. Mastery is the easiest and fastest learning there is, a time when conscious thought is no longer necessary. Once mastered, you can apply it to anything you want to learn.

'When someone masters something, that thing

becomes a part of him. It becomes part of the individual's thinking and creative process. It adds the quality of its essence to all subsequent thoughts and creativity of the individual.'

This part should be treated as a game and an adventure, not a job.

Encouraging and stimulating are key concepts, along with avoiding criticism.

Specifically, The Davis Orientation Protocol teaches dyslexic students how to recognize and control the mental state that leads to distorted and confused perceptions of letters, words and numbers. Through a simple mental technique, students learn to turn off the mental processes that cause the distorted thoughts and reset the mind to a relaxed, focused state suitable for reading and other studies. Once the orientation has been learned, the learner is ready to build the conceptual skills that will enable him or her to overcome the problems arising from dyslexia. It is a rather simple process, almost innate in dyslexics, which allows them to go and develop a faculty they already possess in order to control it. There are just a few tips to follow:

- ❖ Make sure the person is a candidate for the Orientation Protocol by assessing his or her ability to move the mind's eye;

- ❖ Make sure the person wishes to perform the entire process;

- ❖ Maintain a supportive friendly control as you guide the person through the steps;

- ❖ Make sure the person is not tired, not hungry, and not taking any medication that interferes with perception and thinking.

This is followed by the initial protocol session consisting of the greeting and introduction, leading to an initial approach to the person and clarification of concepts.

It also becomes necessary to initiate the process of clarification tuning, a method that serves the oriented dyslexic to have him or she find his or her optimal point of orientation. The name comes from the process of tuning a radio, which is done by moving the dial back and forth until the best reception point is found. The same thing can be done with the mind's eye: by moving it around the orientation point that already exists, one can locate the optimal place for orientation. However, it is necessary to carry out this operation after at least two days of experience have passed since the orientation check and after the disappearance of any lurching.

After this process has been completed, one moves on to ending right/left confusion problems, with Koosh Ball Therapy, given the use of light, fluffy balls made of elastic thread. It is presented in the text as follows:

❖ Place yourself in front of the person at a distance of two to three meters and begin by telling the student to check his or her point, i.e., it must be oriented, balanced on one foot, changing it at any time.

❖ Hold both balls in one hand and when the student is totally balanced on one foot, say, << Grab one ball in one hand and the other ball in the other hand >>

❖ Throw from underneath one ball at a time slowly, aiming at about chest height; each time say << One in one hand, one in the other >>

❖ Repeat, when the student easily catches a ball with either hand without losing balance: << One in one hand, one in the other and throw both >>

4) Epicenter of perception defined by Davis: "If you

close your eyes and look at a mental image, only thought of, the point of perception is that point from which you are looking or that point you use to look." It is not the same point of perception, but it works on the same basic principles as sight: one thing looking at another ... mind's eye which is referred to in dictionaries as imagination, balls simultaneously, aiming at the sundial point in front of the person. When the student grasps them correctly, congratulate him and do it again.

- Say after a while: << I am going to throw them both to one side. Catch them without losing your balance>>. Repeat this for each side so that the student has to cross the center line with his hand to catch both balls. Do not aim too far, or you will make him lose his balance.

After the Orientation Protocol, Symbol Mastery is used to master the alphabet and punctuation. It empowers dyslexic students to think with symbols and words so that they can learn to read with ease and comprehend completely.

Using plasticine, students initially work with the alphabet, numbers, and punctuation marks to ensure that they have the correct perception and understand these symbols. Students then use the plasticine to model the trigger words, those apparent to their eyes, short and abstract, often encountered in reading, such as and, the, a, or and lo. These cause problems when dyslexic students cannot picture a mental image that can connect.

Through Symbol Mastery, students build a three-dimensional plasticine model symbolizing the meaning of each word, along with one in reference to the letters of the words themselves. With this approach, learning is lifelong.

Below are some pictures related to examples of plasticine, used for Symbol Mastery.

In addition to plasticine or clay, other materials needed are vocabulary, grammar, elementary aids, reading books, workbooks, magazines, etc., paper, pencil, scissors, clay modeling tools, materials for cleaning up, and examples of uppercase and lowercase letters.

To this end, the author recommends that we print a page from the book devoted to the alphabet, enlarge it by 150 percent on a photocopier, cut the sheet into three and glue it together to make one long strip.

110 1 1001110011 1111 00110
001
100
00
110
1 0
1
101
011
0
101
000
111
10
11
01
1

4.3 A guide for parents and teachers: how and what they can do?

If we think that the road to learning to read and write is a journey from the city of Language to the city of Reading, then dyslexic people have to use a back road, while others use the highway. It may be that the road is viable, but no one has shown them the way to travel it.

Dyslexic people, in order to reach their destination, discover a different route, and explore new worlds, and new areas; can boldly go where others are afraid to go. He or she may also decide where to go, but they must take the longest route.

The teacher's role is to understand that these children can reveal the distance, but they need help to develop the strategies that will point them on the right course and help them stay on it...If the dyslexic child cannot learn the way we teach, he or she can teach us the way to make him or her learn. Dyslexic individuals can reach their destination if we get them the maps if we explain to them how they are to be used, and if we offer them assistance along the way; but let them be free to see things differently.

This reflection is particularly striking as it confronts us with the problem of the road to success/failure, which every dyslexic, whether a child or an adult, is faced with on their life's journey.

By providing them with the solution to only the problem of the difficulty they 'suffer' from, we resort to mistakes that reverberate in 'self-esteem and failure disastrous for their future and immersion in today's society.

What can we do to safeguard this?

Marshall (information Services Director for Davis Dyslexia Association International) and Shaywitz (Yale University), in their research, confirm that to improve a dyslexic child's learning, we go through alternative strategies. First, if a teacher has doubts about the child's learning, it is advisable to talk about it with colleagues and experts; then it is essential to talk to the family to refer them to a specialized center, explaining to them that, according to the observations made in the classroom, the child's school performance and intelligence do not coincide. In this way, they can be incited and helped to seek help.

Parents of dyslexic children may feel inadequate and

suffer from the situation their child is experiencing; they may be stressed that at ten years old they still cannot tie their shoes and forget where they put things. Important become in this regard, groups of parents who come together not only to try to improve the quality of life of these children but also to confront each other and to support, in turn, those parents who are beginning to enter the world of dyslexia.

Underlying this is the problem of identifying these individuals, which is hindered by three false myths such as the belief, on the part of many teachers, that the gifted child must demonstrate talent in all areas of development; the emphasizing of memory and text comprehension skills, which are not always present in students who have superior abilities in analytical reasoning and creative problem solving; and finally, we find that related to the limited information the teacher has about each student and thus the lack of understanding of the child's learning style and needs. The criterion of discrepancy I mentioned in the first chapter comes in handy here, which turns out to be the main identification key after the specificity and exclusion of other associated disabilities.

It sometimes happens that during interviews, the

children's being particularly bright before entering school emerges, a factor noted by parents, the first recognizers of their strengths and weaknesses. The talent they manifested before entering school, and subsequent failure, can be an important indicator of gifted dyslexic students, and a parent may be the best person to detect this because he or she has a complete view of their child, including extracurricular interests. To find out if your child is learning Visuospatially, you can perform the following questionnaire:

- ❖ Ask what he sees when the word 'dog' is said; the child will say he physically sees a dog;

- ❖ Ask to visualize an elephant, a bird, a refrigerator, a truck and describe it in detail. In the case of visual children they will be able to make a detailed description;

- ❖ Ask the child to describe the house of his favorite friend; the number of details he will remember will be surprising.

For this, it is necessary to schedule group meetings that give the opportunity to socialize, and get to know children who have the same problems and their own potential. Cooperative work is an excellent tool for cognitive development, as well as motivation.

Compensatory strategies become focusing on the child's potential, encouraging the use of compensatory tools such as a calculator, and spell checker on the computer, dispensatory strategies such as reading aloud, reducing the workload; using the blackboard as positive reinforcement; teaching how to use mind maps to organize work respecting physiological rest times.

Providing input on strategies to improve learning, dividing them into three groups, is Whitmore, who talks precisely about:

- ❖ Supportive strategies: based on children's needs and interests, they allow students to bypass a subject in which they have already shown proficiency;
- ❖ Inherent strategies: tend to provoke positive attitudes, encouraging efforts;
- ❖ Remedial strategies: based on the assumption that there is no perfect student and that every child has strengths and weaknesses, as well as different social, emotional, and intellectual needs. In this way, the child will be able to excel in the field in which he is most gifted and see his deficits considered as a normal aspect of learning.

Avoiding making children feel inferior or failed, and supporting their particular talents, becomes an important task of the school, which will increase motivation in learning and give these individuals the experience that other people have confidence in their abilities in various fields, helping them develop a strong and positive identity, making talents available to society.

The creative abilities, intellectual effort, and passion they put into their hobbies are indicators of their potential gifts.

Finally, one must remember not to neglect drawing for note-taking and to use it while studying, to help comprehension and retention of the studied material.

CONCLUSION

And here we come to the end of this book. At the end of a splendid journey.

Summing up the topics covered, an important aspect that contributes to the formation of creative skills is precisely dyslexia, with its many aspects.

Through the creative act, something innovative is produced, which can allow the individual to break out of the constructions of reality, even if temporarily.

Since the child usually presents from an early age an attitude inclined to creativity, it is necessary to intervene from the earliest years of life, letting him totally abandon himself to the course of his ideas, in full freedom of expression, with his own language. An important task, entrusted to education that leads to stimulating and strengthening, is that attitude already present in the child.

It would all seem so easy, when in fact it is not.

And everything is also reflected in the problems experienced by teachers themselves in elementary school, when they have to help dyslexic pupils to continue to express their creative genius, their character, both in the school environment and on the stage of life.

We continue to always praise imagination, never leave it on the back burner, and find new innovative solutions that help the dyslexic child emerge and no longer be afraid in front of a written text.

Great examples and personalities of dyslexic creative geniuses come right from the past, where sculptors, writers, scientists, politicians, and actors. Although they suffered from dyslexia, with their tenacity and courage they managed to move forward and let the creativity they were hiding, slowly emerge, until it became a new discovery.

Now for a moment, I would like us to try to identify ourselves with a typical day, experienced by a dyslexic child in the climate he or she experiences, made up of misunderstandings and difficulties, between school and homework. Let us try to imagine what those what are called 'the carefree years' turn into.

We should not forget that in front of us there is always a helpless child, with his ever-changing personality. Only in this way could we imagine how much his ongoing struggle with dyslexia and his struggle to be understood by the people around him may cost in developmental and self-esteem terms.

I advise you, parents, to always keep in mind that it is not important that your child is first in the class because it means nothing. Instead, remember that what really matters is to be first in life.

This is what a dyslexic child would like to show and communicate to us. What makes the difference, in the face of a problem like dyslexia, is really the will.

I would like to conclude my paper with this reflection from a video, Antonello's Gift, which highlights what has been my treatment.

Antonello is 11 years old and knows that he is different from other children. He takes twice as long to do his homework; reading is a marathon; an addition is a hieroglyphic to decipher. So he gets lost, discouragement assails him and makes him feel stupid. But Antonello is not stupid: quite the contrary.

You should spy on him as he plays by himself: he uses his hands as puppets and improvises theater. He has a wild imagination. Besides, he speaks, writes English, and uses sophisticated words. Every now and then he shoots a funny joke, like the time he was five years old when a lady asked him, <Antonello, what are you doing?>.

And he: <Well, I break my little balls.... >. Antonello is different from other children.

Antonello is dyslexic. Do you know what dyslexia is? A disorder that complicates reading and writing, counting, and learning sequential information (like multiplication tables). Don't that dyslexics are less intelligent, but it compensates by pumping the other, that of visual imagination and other perceptions. My mind takes the highway; Antonello's takes the off-trail, motocross, and jumps. In my brain, the idea enters clothed in letters, and walks straight: in Antonello's brain, the idea is a fantastical animal that slips curiously into a maze of roads; it is iridescent, becomes a comet, and dances with other stars. We see a bright dot; his mind shows him the sky.

No one understands things as a whole better than

dyslexics. Do you know about financial or scientific systems? They go by intuition and get it right; we study and get lost. In short, dyslexics get lost in the simple things, maybe mess up the money accounts at the ice cream parlor, but give us a lead in complex reasoning. They are more curious than average and have vivid imaginations. They hear double, like geniuses. And they could dictate five letters at once, like Napoleon as he mulled over how to invade Russia.

Einstein, Darwin, Edison, Leonardo da Vinci, Michelangelo, Raphael, Van Gogh, Picasso, Beethoven, Mozart, Flaubert, Agatha Christie, Mark Twain, Lewis Carrol, Walt Disney, Julius Verne, Napoleon, Julius Caesar, Roosevelt, Kennedy, George Washington, Churchill. All dyslexic. The majority of scientists at the Massachusetts Institute of Technology are dyslexic. The best surgeons are dyslexic. In America there is this joke going around: 'You have to have surgery? Make sure your surgeon can't spell!'

Antonello? Yes, you are different. You have a gift. I had a friend in college, dyslexic like you, who in order to learn the civil code wrote it down on slips of paper and hung it up around the house. It didn't work. Do you know why? It was opposing his mind. She was pawing at it:

it was a mind for tap, for tango, for tamuré, for exotic, twisted dances. But he wanted to impose the "qua qua" dance on her. Let your imagination run away with you, Antonello. Don't believe it if they make you feel dumb because you are slow in your homework. Your brother is right: those who humiliate dyslexics are mediocre people who think they are special while they are just third-grade beasts. You explain to the teachers that you simply have a different way of learning. Use the calculator, the recorder, and the computer. Use the keyboard and the writing programs. You will see that you can do it. They say you are very strong with new technology. Don't give up, okay? And write your first e-mail. On your own. Type in your identity: Antonello is outstanding.

Thank you for getting to the end of the book, I have spent a lot of time writing the manuscript and I ask you to help me with the dissemination of the book. It would be very helpful if you would leave me a positive review on AMAZON. Thank you very much!

Thank you!!!!

Being dyslexic can actually help in the outside world. I see some things clearer than other people do because I have to simplify things to help me and that has helped others.

Richard Branson

Creativity is the key for any child with dyslexia, or for anyone for that matter. Then you can think outside of the box. Teach them anything is attainable. Let them run with what you see is whatever they need to run with.

Orlando Bloom

His teachers said that he was mentally slow, unsociable, and adrift in his foolish dreams.

Albert Einstein

Being diagnosed with Dyslexia at age 60 was "like the last puzzle past in a tremendous mystery that I've kept to myself all these years."

Steven Spielberg

I failed in some subjects in exam, but my friend passed in all. Now he is an engineer for Microsoft and I am the owner of Microsoft.

Bill Gates

One Problem with the way the educational system is set up is that is only recognizes a certain type of intelligence, and it's incredibly restrictive -very, very restrictive. There's so many types of intelligence, and people who would be at their best outside of that structure get lost.

Bruce Springsteen

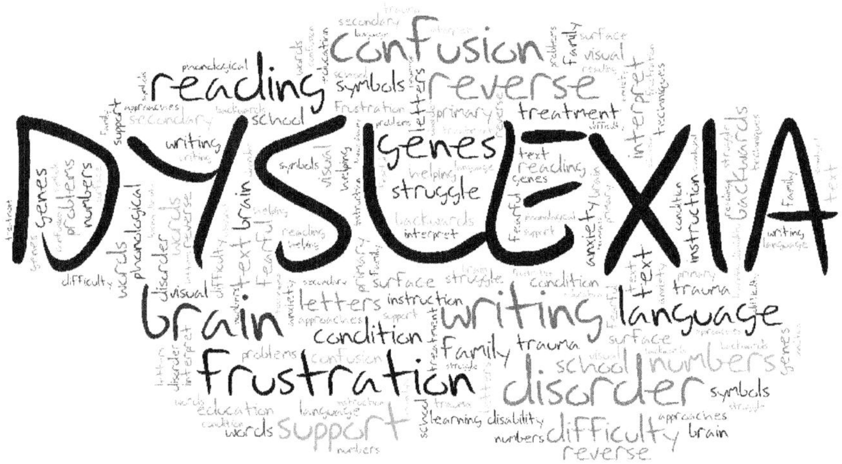
DYSLEXIA
confusion
reading
reverse
genes
struggle
treatment
interpret
backwards
brain
writing
language
frustration
disorder
numbers
difficulty
support
condition
family
trauma
school
letters
symbols
education
learning disability
anxiety
instruction
surface
words
phonological
problems
visual
text
fearful

BIBLIOGRAPHY

Parents Association, Primo Levidi Bollate, Dyslexia, comeseguirel'ondagiusta, Libraccio Editore, Milan, 2014.

AA.VV, Dyslexia and other DSA at school, Erickson, Trento, Italy, 2013.

American Psychiatric Association, DSM-IV-TR, Diagnostic and statistical manual of mental disorders, Elsevier, Milan, 2000.

DSM- IV, Diagnostic and statistical manual of mental disorders, Masson, Milan 1992.

E. Benso, Dyslexia, The Green Lion, Turin 2011.

G. Stella, L. Grandi, Comeleggere la Dlessia e i DSA, Giunti Scuola, Florence 2011. Giacomo Stella, Dyslexia, Il Mulino, 2004.

Giacomo Stella, In the classroom with a student with

learning disorders, Milan, Fabbri, 2001. Giacomo Stella and Enrico Savelli, Dyslexia today, Erickson, Trento, Italy, 2012.

ICD-10, Tenth Revision of the International Classification of Psychological and Behavioral Syndromes and Disorders, Masson, Milan 1992.

Law No. 170, October 8, 2010, 'Official Gazette' 244, October 18, 2010.

Guidelines attached to the 'Ministerial Decree' July 12, 2011. Maryanne Wolf, We are not born to read.

Maryanne Wolf, Proust the squid, Vitae Pensiero, 2009. Pirro Ugo, Miofigliononon sa leggere, Rizzoli, Milan 1981.

Ronald D. Davis, The gift of dyslexia, why some very smart people cannot read and how they can learn, Armando Editore, Ronciglione, 2010.

Rossella Grenci, Eagles were born to fly. The creative genius in dyslexic children, Erickson, Trento, 2015.

Printed in Great Britain
by Amazon

18285250R00072